Life's Simple Pleasures

■ ■ ■

Edited by Rod Guge

Copyright © 1993, Great Quotations Publishing Company

Edited by Rod Guge

Cover Design by Julie Otlewis

Page Design and Typesetting by Bostrom Publishing, Inc.

Printed in Hong Kong

Acknowledgements

The responses presented in Life's Simple Pleasures have been contributed by people of all ages, all backgrounds and all 50 states. Since America is a melting pot of opinions and thoughts, the goal of this ongoing project is to produce a book series that presents a rainbow of thoughts -- thoughts that make you laugh, some that prompt a tear, some that challenge your way of thinking, and maybe a few that inspire you to throw the book across the room.

When we take time to understand each other, then we're each doing our part to make America a better place. If this book series can help achieve that -- even to a small degree -- then it has been worth all the time and effort it took to develop.

Thanks so much to all the folks on these pages who took the time and effort to share how they feel.

Josh Max, Dorothy Elliott, A.C. Ramsey, Alan Sparrow, Brandon Castor, Paige Leitman, B. Wittelsberger, Steve Goodman, Dawn Matschke, Tiffany Graetz, Dee Southwood Blakey, Cynthia Felty, Ed Castor, John Paul Spiridakis, David A. Elizondo, Dennis McGrath, M. Setlock, David Simons, Uncle Junky, Barbara Miedema, Becki Fogle, Kent Alexander, Jack D'Alelio, An Bartel, Amy Fong, Jenny Palmer, Zac Willette, Amy Rutkowski, Brooke Craig, Karen Butenko, Caren Lissner, Megan Lissner, Steven Trujillo, Karen Dorsett, Andrea Defusco, Laura Stride, Carmen Kunze, Lawrence J. Pippick, L. Houle Gutierrez, Carole Vance, Phaedra Sharpe, Wayne Barnes, Marissa Maciel, Michael Blau, Patrick Robbins, T. Wolf Bolz, Kristyn Shaffer, Stephen Meyer, Dawn K. Gupta, Tallie Conner, David Ziegenhagen, Perrin Patterson, L.L. Baldwin, Randall Cook, Barbara Affrunti, Josh Modell, Roy Henock, Harlen Walsh, Nancy Peters, Connie Auer, Grace Andrus, Sandra Lynn Sabo, Robert Phillip O'dell, Kevin Miller, Mary Bieber, Linda O'Connell, Ginger Sharp Brown, Terry Brown, Kayci Rothweiler, Connie Johnson, Walt Wentz, Jim Knauff, Ginny Knauff, Jeremy Knauff, James Knauff, Jordan Knauff, Ward S. Krause, Louise Sullivan, Bob Brunner, Nancy C. Barnes, Sharon Boone, Robin Conover, Cathleen Cope, Diane Gahner, Wanda Conley, Teresa Garland, Kimberly Long, Heather Berry, John Kirby, Greg Kingdon, Forrest Bradley, Ken Astrup, Susan Pegden, Bill Perry, Lynn Bartlett, James V. Chambers, Teres Lambert, Terri R. Taylor-Hamrick, Karl W. Hockmeyer, Myrna Dossert, Myron Casey, Lee Chamblee, Beth Byron, Kathy Hayes, Suzanne Gordon, Gordon Gee, Lesa Taylor, Maryann Fosby, Neil Christiansen, Ashley Guge, Tyler Guge, Julie Murfitt, Kathy Penry, Pam Brunet, Anna Harbourt, Ann Geiszler, T.C. Whitehurst, Meredith Libbey, Randolph Melick, Linda Cochran, Tom Harmon, Ramona Mackenroth, Pam Karg, Jean Reid, Patrick Sharp.

It makes me happy ...

To find out people think I'm naturally blonde.

-- Legal clerk and former model (F), Age 31, Utah

■ ■ ■

What makes us happy?

Tuning in for an episode of The Simpsons and finding out that it's not a re-run.

-- Chemist (M), Age 37, Massachusetts

■ ■ ■

When I don' t have a cavity.

-- Student (M), Age 8 1/2, Texas

It makes me happy ...

When my mother is happy.

When my mother-in-law is despondent.

-- *Sales manager (M), Age 50, Alabama*

■ ■ ■

It makes us happy ...

To know that no innocent animals were sacrificed in
the making of a Sara Lee Cheesecake.

-- Singer & word processor (F), Age 35, New Mexico

■ ■ ■

To eat a lot of chocolate.

-- Communications coordinator (F), Age 27, New York

What makes me happy?

Being appreciated.

Being with my friends.

Being thinner than my sister.

-- Owner/operator of a plant maintenance service (F), Age 44, California

■ ■ ■

It makes me happy ...

To get all dressed up for an evening on the town.

To take everything back off the second I get home.

-- Rehabilitation consultant, nursing (F), Age 50, Ohio

■ ■ ■

It makes me happy ...

When I speed through radar and don't get a ticket.

When the Atlanta Braves win.

When the Democrats lose.

When we bomb Iraq.

-- Sales manager (M), Age 45, Alabama

■ ■ ■

It makes me happy ...

When I ask my mother, "Which daughter am I?"
and she gets my name right on the first try.

To find something special to buy someone
that they want or collect.

When I do a good job and someone notices.

-- Reigstered nurse and director of eduction (F), Age 31, California

■ ■ ■

It makes me happy ...

When I get to ride horses with my grand-dad.

To eat my mom's lasagna.

To help somebody when I can.

-- Student (F), Age 10, Iowa

■ ■ ■

It makes me happy …

To have a clean desk at work,
although I don't remember the last time that happened.

When I come home and have five messages
on my answering machine.

When all those messages aren't from my mother …

When I go to family reunions and everybody doesn't ask me when am I ever going to get married.

When I sit and realize that, all things considered, I'm really pretty happy.

-- Photojournalist (F), Age 31, Pennsylvania

■ ■ ■

It makes me happy …

To stop smoking for more than a day.

To know that, chances are, my neighbor's yappy little obnoxious dog, which I hate, cannot live to be much older than 13, and it just turned 12.

When I try a new recipe and it comes out looking
like the picture in the cookbook.

When the video I almost didn't rent
turns out to be a great movie,
even though I had never heard of it
and it was in an ugly box.

-- Research technician (F), Age 37, Nebraska

■ ■ ■

It makes me happy ...

To sing at the top of my lungs in the car.

To find out I have one more cigarette in a pack
that I thought was empty.

To realize that I'm not afraid to make a fool of myself if that's what it takes to try and reach for my dreams.

To think about getting a recording deal one day.

-- Aspiring country music singer (M), Age 32, Tennessee

■ ■ ■

Here's what makes me happy ...

A warm spring day ...
Attention from the opposite sex ...
My MAC ... A good song title ... Driving ... Sushi ...
Hearing my girlfriend call my name in the morning ...
Getting paid in cash ... Getting up early ...
Walking into a clean apartment ...

... Giving someone a surprise ... Getting mail ... Getting on the scale and having it read less than what I expected ... A new haircut ... Reading good news in the paper ... Plants ... Bugs Bunny ... The Simpsons ... Applause ...

These make me happy, too ...

... Touching ground in an airplane ... Seeing a fat woman
eat an ice cream cone unabashedly ... Rollerblading ...
A smile from the bank teller or the checkout clerk ...
Anytime when someone listens ... Doing someone a favor ...
Getting a message ... Writing to people I don't know.

-- Singer/songwriter/musician/writer/painter (M), Age 31, New York

■ ■ ■

It makes me happy ...

To be the only unmarried, childless sibling so that I can teach all my nieces and nephews how to emit disgusting bodily noises, which seriously annoys and embarrasses their parents (my siblings), which is fun for me.

To get that rare but exhilarating sense of accomplishment that can only come from having scrubbed my bathroom.

-- Federal health agency information research specialist (F), Age 32, Maryland

■ ■ ■

What makes me happy?

Jazz … The Guiding Light … Indian art …
Coffee … a view … friends and family.

-- Manager (F), Age 47, Virginia

■ ■ ■

It makes me happy ...

To watch the sun set in the mountains.

When my windshield wipers work during downpours.

When I can see my closet floor.

-- Benefits consultant (F), Age 28, Connecticut

■ ■ ■

It makes me happy ...

To think that one day women and men will be paid
equally for doing the same job under the same conditions,
and with comparable effectiveness. For this to happen
in my lifetime would be even better.

-- Teacher (F), Age 44, Mississippi

■ ■ ■

It makes me happy ...

When the batteries aren't dead.

When my answering machine doesn't cut
the last four digits off the message.

When the "In" stack is less than 8 inches tall.

-- Photographer (F), Age 27, Arizona

■ ■ ■

It makes me happy ...

To spend an hour or so in the evening
snuggling with my husband, just the two of us,
in front of the TV, with no interruption.

To start out on a vacation.

To come back home ...

To hold hands with my husband
during the sermon on Sunday mornings.

To realize my family is healthy.

To be able to work a part-time job.

-- Dental assistant (F), Age 45, North Dakota

■ ■ ■

When I'm about to make some terrible mistake
in the laundromat and some nice lady I've never seen
stops me and tells me how to do it right.

To see poor people get a break in life …

When my niece and nephew come to stay
for a week with me during the summer.

When they go home.

When I hear that the person who just won
millions in the Florida lottery
had worked two jobs for years just to get by.

-- *Studio camera technician (M), Age 27, Idaho*

■ ■ ■

It makes me happy ...

When I finish something ahead of the deadline.

When I get recognized for things I've done.

When I think about how much my family loves me.

-- College student (F), Age 19, Kansas

■ ■ ■

It makes me happy ...

To watch the accomplishments at the Special Olympics.

To have someone guess my age younger than I am.

To see rude people put in their place.

-- Administrative assistant (F), Age 50, Wyoming

■ ■ ■

These things make us happy ...

When I get excited about something I've just learned,
whether it's in the classroom, through travel, through museum
visits or through simple observations of life.

-- College Spanish major (F), Age 22, Michigan

■ ■ ■

When I see my little tomboy squeeze herself into her tutu.

-- Department store buyer (F), Age 31, Washington, D.C.

To sell lots of old junk at a yard sale.

To pick up more junk at somebody else's yard sale.

-- Part-time dental assistant and full-time mother
with a station wagon (F), Age 43, Vermont

■ ■ ■

It makes me happy ...

To curl up on the couch on a snowy Saturday
and watch old movies all day long.

To start an exercise program
and actually stick with it for awhile ...

To give my family things they truly want for Christmas.

To start a project at work before the last minute.

To have the columns add up at the end.

-- Accountant (F), Age 51, Virginia

■ ■ ■

It makes me happy ...

To run across a department store sale that lets me take an additional 50 percent off the Lowest Marked Price.

It makes me even happier if the thing I just bought on sale is something I can actually use (makes my husband happy, too.)

-- Homemaker and shopping fanatic (F), Age 42, Louisiana

■ ■ ■

It makes me happy ...

To see through some scheme designed
to part me from my money.

-- Corporate controller (M), Age 46, Indiana

■ ■ ■

It makes me happy …

When, despite the chaos
that is my organizational system,
I know exactly where something is.

When I'm with my 127 cousins …

When I'm having a less-than-desirable-kind-of-day
and I look outside and the clouds, the sun
and the trees are all dancing.

When I make a difference in some small way.

When I teach.

-- Education student (M), Age 19, Minnesota

■ ■ ■

It makes me happy ...

When I find a parking place
right by the entrance to the store.

When I get together with friends from college.

When I'm with people who can talk politics at dinner
and nobody throws anything.

When I can relax, knowing I never have
to go back to school again if I don't want to.

-- Attorney (F), Age 29, Michigan

■ ■ ■

It makes me happy ...

When I wear my Mickey Mouse socks.

When my husband and I go out on a Dairy Queen date.

To enjoy a warm cup of cocoa on a cold winter day.

When I go to sleep at night and know that God is still awake.

When my nieces and nephews would rather be with me
than with their other aunts and uncles.

When I am awakened at night by my husband
covering me up with the blankets he's been hogging.

-- Typesetter (F), Age 27, North Dakota

■ ■ ■

It makes me happy …

When I wake up in the morning
thinking I'm late for work
and then realize it's Saturday.

When I finally complete a project -- any project!

When the bathtub is clean.

When the car starts.

When I can find the remote control for the TV.

When people remember to call.

-- Speechwriter (F), Age 29, Rhode Island

■ ■ ■

It makes me happy …

When my sons do not get a progress report from school.

When all my family members are home at night
and we say "good night" to each other.

To watch people place their hands
over their hearts and stand when the flag passes
or the national anthem is played.

To hear raindrops on a tin roof.

-- Salesman (M), Age 40, Texas

■ ■ ■

45

It makes me happy ...

To buy gaudy earrings.

To spell a hard name correctly
when I'm taking information over the phone.

-- Airline reservations supervisor (F), Age 42, North Dakota

■ ■ ■

It makes me happy ...

To have time and freedom to create.

To associate with creative people.

To be out in the woods or on the water.

-- Magazine editor (M), Age 51, Oregon

■ ■ ■

It makes us happy ...

When my older brother lets me play Nintendo.

-- Middle brother of three, Age 8, Georgia

■ ■ ■

When my baby sitter be's nice to me.

-- Younger brother of three, Age 4, Georgia

■ ■ ■

When I go to sleep, because I'm not worried
about anything and my brothers aren't fighting.

-- Younger brother of three, Age 4, Georgia

It makes us happy ...

When I feel physically able to meet everyone's needs, including my own.

-- Homemaker and mother of three, Age 36, Georgia

■ ■ ■

When the whole family is getting along.

-- Hotel director and father of three, Age 45, Georgia

It makes me happy ...

When I eat White Castles ... When I hear good
old-fashioned gossip ... When I'm nasty to other people
who deserve it ... When I win at cards or bingo ...
When I listen to Elvis and Billy Ray Cyrus tapes.

-- Administrative assistant (F), Age 46, Minneosta

■ ■ ■

It makes me happy ...

When I can beat my boyfriend at anything --
which is almost never.

To read the "Cathy" comic strip because I relate well to her.

To have a car with air conditioning.

-- *Magazine writer (F), Age 25, Kentucky*

■ ■ ■

It makes me happy ...

When the conversation and the candlelight
last as long as the romance.

When my sweetheart learns to cook, dance or enjoy foreign
movies because I enjoy cooking, dancing and foreign movies.

When people do the right thing.

-- Bank Vice President (F), Age 32, Tennesee

■ ■ ■

It makes me happy ...

When I wake up to sunshine in the morning.

When my grandchildren come to visit.

When I go to work, because I thoroughly enjoy my job.

-- Secretary to the Governor (F), Age 56, Montana

■ ■ ■

It makes me happy ...

When the paint chips actually match
the color in the can.

To think about going to Europe on vacation
sometime before the world comes to an end.

To hear Louis Armstrong sing
"What a Wonderful World" ...

To hear that people I can't stand
are suffering personal hardships.

To know that, no matter how bad things sometimes get,
I can always count on the fact that "This, too, shall pass."

-- Promotions director (M), Age 32, Tennessee

■ ■ ■

It makes me happy …

To wake up in the morning with the same
number of wrinkles I went to bed with.

To know that I have a dog who will love me
no matter how miserably I fail …

To share my M&M's and to keep
all the green ones for myself.

To have three bowls of ice cream in secret
while I'm on a diet.

To see a little baby's naked bottom and cute little toes.

-- Student (F), Age 19, Georgia

■ ■ ■

It makes me happy ...

To still fit into a 10-year-old pair of jeans
without having to lie on a bed to zip them up.

To know that for a gringo,
I make an enchilada <u>muy bueno</u> ...

To know that I have never belted a sales clerk
for suggesting I'd look great in black or vertical stripes.

To know that I help lots of people have a good time
just by doing what I love to do most
(while getting paid to do it!)

-- Night club performer (F), Age 34, Nevada

■ ■ ■

It makes me happy ...

To know that a genius still exists.

To know that objectivism is not dead,
only a little hard to find.

To know that intelligent men
are out there somewhere ...

When I find a pair of jeans that not only fit
but look good. At least until I wash them.

When I'm rowing an eight-person shell, full power,
in sync with seven other people, across glass-like water
as the sun is rising. What a trip!

-- *Student and women's crew team member (F), Age 20, Oklahoma*

■ ■ ■

61

It makes me happy ...

When my pantyhose last longer than a day.

When my children laugh
(but not at the runs in my pantyhose.)

-- Association management administrator (F), Age 32, Virginia

■ ■ ■

What makes me happy?

When my dog, Megan, senses that I'm sad
and nuzzles against me.

-- Temp worker (looking for a job in communication) (F),
Age 22, New Jersey

■ ■ ■

Lying in the sun and getting my stomach rubbed.

-- House pet (aka Megan) (F), Age 8 (or 56 in dog years),
as interpreted by owner, New Jersey

What makes me happy?

Seeing a month pass without one of my current
or former students in Salinas, California,
become a drive-by shooting victim.

-- High school teacher/counselor (M), Age 40, California

■ ■ ■

What makes us happy?

Eating string cheese while watching "Beverly Hills 90210."

-- College student (F), Age 19, Ohio

■ ■ ■

Trimming the Christmas tree with all the wonderful
and silly mementos of years and lives past.

-- Corporate administrator and ex-dancer (M), Age 37, Iowa

What makes me happy?

The way Keith Richards plays guitar.

Luciano Pavarotti …

Cities at Christmastime.

Christopher Plummer in *The Sound of Music*.

Rain at night.

-- *English professor (F), Age 25, Massachusetts*

■ ■ ■

It makes me happy?

When my children don't fight.

When my kids come home beaming,
with all A's on their report cards ...

When my wife and I make love.

When I go hunting or fishing.

When the Twins win.

-- Co-op director (M), Age 41, North Dakota

■ ■ ■

It makes me happy ...

When my granddaughter tells me I'm pretty.

To run into old friends in unexpected places.

To babysit with my grandchildren
and have them all to myself.

When I think about being married
to the same man for 38 years.

-- *Homemaker (F), Age 58, Kentucky*

■ ■ ■

It makes me happy ...

To be part of a youth program
that is a positive influence on young people.

Knowing that there are things to be happy about
when we are surrounded by negative distractions.

-- Salesman (M), Age 40, Texas

■ ■ ■

It makes me happy ...

To make my wife and family happy.

To get together with my best friends
on the golf course and beat them mercilessly.

-- Retired law enforcement officer (M), Age 74, Illinois

■ ■ ■

It makes me happy ...

When I spend time with my teenage sons
and we actually talk about everyday, normal events.

To trim my rosebushes,
knowing the beautiful flowers will be my reward.

To see someone wearing a garment
that looks good and really fits.

When I come out of the beauty shop
with a haircut that isn't too short!

-- Teacher (F), Age 43, Arizona

■ ■ ■

It makes me happy ...

For my children to get older
and finally realize I knew what I was talking about.

To get a debt paid off.

What makes us happy?

To have money left over
when the next paycheck comes.

To go home, to my own little
place in the world, after work.

-- Power company employee (M), Age 59, Missouri

■ ■ ■

It makes me happy …

When my cash journal balances.

When I get a good raise in salary.

To hit the jackpots on the
slot machine in Vegas.

To win in Vegas even though
I'm Church of Christ.

-- Deputy clerk (F), Age 50, Tennessee

■ ■ ■

It makes me happy ...

When 4:00 p.m. comes 'round on a Friday.

When I get a great haircut
(to make up for the lousy one I got last time).

When it isn't raining and the sun
is actually shining in Seattle.

When my significant other sets out candles
and makes an ordinary dinner into a romantic event.

-- Patient account representative (M), Age 30, Washington

■ ■ ■

It makes me happy ...

When I get my allowance.

When it snows.

When I get to go get the mail.

When school is over.

-- *Student (M), Age 8, New Jersey*

■ ■ ■

What makes me happy?

The pursuit of enlightenment in the humblest sense
possible. It is not about puffing cigarettes and behaving
like a pseudo-intellectual, but about taking each day
and using it in some new way. When I go to sleep at night
a tad wiser than when I awoke that morning,
I know that it was a good day …

Some days are filled with good fortune and some days are filled with misfortune. What is most important, though, is whether or not I grow from the events at hand. To grow is to become more enlightened, and to be enlightened is to be happy in the innermost sense of the word. To think that I will become enlightened enough to leave this planet in a little better state than when I arrived makes me happy.

-- Wilderness trip leader for teenagers (F), Age 27, Montana

■ ■ ■

What makes us happy?

<u>SPY</u> Magazine.

-- Mail room attendant, non-violent (M), Age 26, Maine

■ ■ ■

To think that one day somebody will get
Pat Robertson and other hatemongers off the tube.

-- Convention planner (M), Age 34, Washington, D.C.

What makes us happy?

Any show not featuring Arsenio Hall.

-- Producer & free spirit (M), Age 46, California

■ ■ ■

Running into country music stars in the Nashville airport.

-- Flight attendant (M), Age 27, Tennessee

What makes me happy?

Driving into one of the major cities in the state,
seeing a blanket of mustard-colored smog
hugging the horizon, and pretending it's fog and that
this is actually a beautiful coastal city …

When a slip of the finger on the channel changer
accidentally puts me face-to-face, so to speak,
with the inimitable Rush Limbaugh blabbering
at great length about President Clinton's loose morals,
and in a blast of gratitude for the miracles of technology,
I realize I can whisk away this Jabba the Hut in a suit
with a simple gesture involving one finger …

What else makes me happy?

The time between the day a new home
with fabulous mountain views is bought
and the moment, seven days later,
that construction is begun on a new house
right across the street ...

Having weathered the decades,
scared of turning 40 for 39 years,
and then when the day finally arrives,
realizing that the party's just begun.

*-- International newspaper humor columnist waiting for the big break,
which means being asked to write for a national publication
or television show (M), Age 40, Arizona*

■ ■ ■

What makes us happy?

Bowling.

-- Business Owner (F), Age 46, Tennessee

■ ■ ■

When my husband and I are driving together
and the radio plays "our song."

-- Church secretary (F), Age 31, New Hampshire

What makes me happy?

Days when my thighs don't rub together.

-- Hotel administrator (F),
Age, like weight, is nobody's business, Michigan

■ ■ ■

It makes me happy ...

To get a free wash with a fill-up.

To finish my workout at the gym ...

To see a groom cry at his wedding.

To see the father of the bride cry at his daughter's wedding.

To sing at weddings (I've done 99 so far)
in which people cry because they're happy.

*-- Law office computer specialist
and part-time wedding vocalist (M), Age 32, Hawaii*

■ ■ ■

What makes us happy?

Seeing children of all walks of life
playing together and learning together.

-- Writer (M), Age ??, Michigan

■ ■ ■

Seeing older people out traveling and living it up.

-- Physician's assistant (M), Age 28, Louisiana

It makes me happy ...

When my husband offers to make up
the baby bottles for the next day.

When I don't have to iron what I want to wear to work,
especially if I'm running late ...

-- Executive secretary (F), Age 28, New York

■ ■ ■

What makes me happy?

Watching people being walked by horrendous dogs,
and yet trying to maintain their composure.

Watching "Mr. Roger's Neighborhood"
on a rainy afternoon while sick at home.

-- *Student (F), Age 16, California*

■ ■ ■

What makes me happy?

Seeing politicians age before my very eyes,
followed closely by seeing self-righteous "ministers"
caught in a sex scandal.

-- Graduate student (M), Age 24, New Hampshire

■ ■ ■

What makes me happy?

Coming up with the "I shoulda said" line
precisely when I need it.

Finding really good clothes
for a ridiculously cheap price …

Much-deserved success, especially when it
follows people predicting utter failure.

Daily reaffirmations of friendships.

"Schoolhouse Rock."

-- Aspiring writer (i.e., unemployed) (M), Age 22, Maine

■ ■ ■

What makes me happy?

Knowing that since the world is going to pot,
things will only get worse after I die.
Also, raw oatmeal with milk and lots of sugar at about 3 a.m.

*-- Professional photographer who moved out of New York, moved out of L.A.,
did not vote for Bill Clinton but did vote for H. Ross Perot since he, too,
is one of the first-name challenged who has only an initial
instead of a real first name (M), Age 39, North Carolina*

■ ■ ■

It makes me happy ...

When there are fewer than 10 news stories
about murder, death, suicide, etc., on the nightly news.

-- Student-soon-to-be-teacher (F), Age 21, New Jersey

■ ■ ■

What makes me happy?

Though it's a rough world out there,
the following things never fail me:

Woody Allen movies;
seeing re-runs of Ronald Reagan acting out
his greatest role as our President;
Jack Nicholson's famed diner scene in "Five Easy Pieces";
John Belushi's gross-out scene in "Animal House" …

Listening to "Rhapsody in Blue" by Gershwin.

Finding out that the time on my parking meter has expired while realizing that I slid by without getting a ticket!

-- Producer & writer (M), Age ??, California

■ ■ ■

It makes me happy ...

When I have days when there's absolutely nothing
that I have to do.

-- Student of molecular biology and chemistry (F), Age 20, Delaware

■ ■ ■

It makes me happy ...

To watch Country Music Television
videos while I work.

-- Housekeeper (F), Age 34, Mississippi

■ ■ ■

It makes me happy ...

To see a student walking through campus
reading a letter and laughing out loud.

When my class is cancelled for no reason at all
and it's a sunny afternoon.

-- English major (F), Age 19, California

■ ■ ■

It makes me happy ...

To sleep with my cat.

To drive my Miata on a sunny day or a warm night.

-- Health care executive (M), Age 56, Minnesota

■ ■ ■

It makes me happy ...

To eat a smushed peanut butter-and-jelly sandwich
atop a big rock after a long hike.

To wake up in the middle of the night, look at my alarm clock,
and realize I still have at least three hours to sleep.

-- Human development student (M), Age 20, Texas

■ ■ ■

It makes me happy ...

When my baby sleeps all night.

When my 2-year-old son eats.

When presentations go well and get the intended response.

-- Public relations executive (F), Age 34, Florida

■ ■ ■

What makes me happy?

I don't often think about happiness. This is mainly
because I was raised in the Catholic faith
where happiness isn't allowed. Filled with original sin,
Catholic girls don't deserve happiness and, if by chance,
happiness comes our way, we'd better feel guilty about it.
However, as I reach middle age, I've put enough distance
between myself and the Church to enable me to feel,
on occassion, a twinge of -- dare I say it -- happiness ...

This phenomena usually occurs in the morning with the dawn of a fresh new day, quiet and still. This almost never fails to cause happiness to well in my heart -- a feeling, however fleeting, that, at least at this moment, all is right with the world. An autumn morning in Connecticut makes me happiest. I love the reds and yellows of the trees emerging through the mist, the cries of birds heading South, a cup of strong, black coffee, a heavy sweater and a walk in the woods. What more could the soul require?

-- Registered nurse in labor & delivery (F), Age 39, Florida

■ ■ ■

What makes me happy?

Grits.

Rush Limbaugh's voting record.

The startling success of "Last Action Hero" …

The fact that South Carolina's first black
Miss South Carolina, Kimberly Aiken,
won Miss America.

Sweetened iced tea at dusk.

*-- Teacher -- just finished two-year teaching contract in Japan,
currently resting (M), Age 24, South Carolina*

■ ■ ■

What makes me happy?

This seems to change with the times and with my
life circumstances. During the '60s (early days),
race equality, peace on earth and women's rights were very
high on my list. Then, as I began to raise my children,
I was happy that each night as they went to bed,
they were healthy and happy and that was enough …

By the mid-70s, my husband became sick
and what made me happy then was just getting
through the illness with some kind of hope of recovery.
By the '80s, my kids were raised and very adjusted,
and my husband had recovered.
I was extremely happy for those things alone ...

Now I'm 50 years old. My family is still well.
The children are married and have children of their own.
My husband is still healthy and working at a good job.
My mom and sisters are all well. Although there is not yet
peace on earth or gender equality, I don't seem to think
of these things much anymore …

I thank God each day for all the blessings, and although I still hope and pray for social change, I don't dwell on these things like I did. I've reached an age at which I now think of myself, something I haven't done most of my life. And I find that the things that now make me happy are friends, and good times, and fun. And laughter. And dancing. I don't have all those things right now, because we just moved here from New York. So it makes me happy that the questionnaire gave me something to do this afternoon.

-- Wife, mother, aunt, sister, mom-in-law, daughter, daughter-in-law, friend, confidant & sales lady looking for a job (F), Age 50, Florida

■ ■ ■

What makes me happy?

Music.

Seeing other people happy.

Absolute silence.

-- Full-time student, full-time record store slave (M), Age 29, Wisconsin

■ ■ ■

What makes me happy?

Getting to do what I really want to do, like playing with my computer, playing chess, or having a sublime physical encounter, not necessarily in this stated order of preference.

-- Jump roll operator in a sawmill, a position that invites city slickers to spend sleepless nights wondering what that really is (M), Age 42, California

■ ■ ■

What makes me happy?

Moments of self-righteous indignation. Whenever, I see
that once again the mighty have fallen -- a stockbroker
carted off to prison, for example, or a television evangelist
caught with his pants down, literally, or whenever
a next-door "Leave It To Beaver" neighbor
is revealed as a multiple maniac mass murderer …

… little bit better off for having revealed such hidden sleaze, as if I had been vindicated for living such a comparatively moral life of open perversion, alcohol and substance abuse, and high-vaulted, alternative, cutting-edge dance music. As my grandmother used to say, "It's better to have nothing to hide than to live in a glass house."

-- Systems analyst (M), Age 37, Massachusetts

■ ■ ■

What makes me happy?

It makes me happy to know that there are actually more things that make me happy than those that make me unhappy. I feel joy watching my daughter sleep and seeing her awake with a smile on her face. I feel happy when I hear the strains of music by Gershwin, or when I hear Barbra Streisand sing anything ... or when I look into the eyes of the man I love or hear his voice on the other end of an answered telephone ...

... I feel happy watching a movie that makes me figure out something in my own life ... or watching and listening to a performance of any Shakespeare play, absorbing the enriching language and learning life's lessons ... but I am happiest remembering the joy I felt the morning I gave birth to my beautiful child -- it will <u>always</u> be the single most ecstatic moment I've ever experienced.

-- Marketing administrator for a major computer conglomerate, single mother of a 6 1/2-year-old daughter, college graduate and Christian (F), Age ??, California

■ ■ ■

What makes us happy?

A loving, close knit family, my faith,
good health, and living in America.

-- Housewife and volunteer, in the process of re-education (F), Age 42, South Dakota

■ ■ ■

Being around a bunch of excited,
exuberant, uninhibited teenagers.

-- Benefits administrator (M), Age 35, Iowa

What makes me happy?

God's answers to my prayers.

-- Nursing home resident (F), Age 85, South Dakota

■ ■ ■

What makes me happy?

Inhaling: as in, I'm so grateful I can still do it
without the assistance of a machine.

*-- 37-year-old grandmother who earns a living cleaning other
people's toilets while attending school full-time, Maine*

■ ■ ■

What makes me happy?

I don't know.
I haven't found her yet.

-- Front desk manager/administrative assistant
(I work two jobs) (M), Age 24, California

■ ■ ■

What makes me happy?

A day in which I have done some serious writing --
even if it's seriously funny.

-- Printing plant worker (M), Age 34, Illinois

■ ■ ■

What makes me happy?

Watching the Star Wars trilogy
and then becoming aware of the magic around me.
Call it "the force" if you want to;
call it karma; call it God.

-- Student (F), Age 19, Arkansas

■ ■ ■

It makes me happy ...

To travel, travel, travel.

To see my children happy,
to be in love, and to give.

-- Corporate buyer (F), Age 47, Tennessee

■ ■ ■

It makes me happy ...

When my husband helps with the dishes.

When music gives me chill bumps,
or when I hear the ocean surf.

When I'm on Broadway at Times Square.

-- Service organization manager (F), Age 32, Tennessee

■ ■ ■

It makes me happy ...

To find a pair of shoes I've been coveting
marked down 50 percent.

To hear one of my co-workers say, "Oh, but I
already buy my Avon from Kathy."

To know that at my age,
I can still get whistled at on the street ...

When my husband comes back early from a
business trip to Florida just because he missed me.

To see my daughter performing in the marching band.

To stand in the mirror and see that the weight
I took off six years ago has stayed off ever since.

-- Legal secretary (F), Age 46, Virginia

■ ■ ■

It makes me happy ...

When my children come by for a visit,
even a short one.

To give encouragement to someone
who has more pain than I.

To play bridge and other games with my friends ...

When my 17-year-old grandson confides in me.

To watch sports on TV with my husband.

To be alive and feeling well.

-- *Senior citizen (F), Age 81, Texas*

■ ■ ■

It makes me happy ...

When the phone rings and I realize that the cordless
is sitting right there on the sofa next to me,
so I don't even have to get up.

When telephone sales people are courteous
enough to ask if they've called at a bad time
before they go into their whole, long-winded speech
about something I don't want ...

When I hear groups of people taking an interest in an election and discussing who might be the best candidate to vote for.

When the maid comes every Friday.

When patients who would otherwise be <u>impatient</u> realize that I'm not as young as I used to be.

-- Registered nurse (F), Age 57, Delaware

■ ■ ■

It makes me happy ...

When an attractive woman
still glances my way.

When I remember all the words
to a favorite '50's song.

When a crisp apple SNAPS open
when I bite into it ...

When my underwear doesn't shrink in the wash.

When skirts get shorter again.

When my blood test comes out okay.

-- Deputy press secretary (M), Age 36, West Virginia

■ ■ ■

It makes me happy ...

When what goes around comes around.

To cry or laugh uncontrollably during a great movie.

When the "do" does, without a hairdryer.

-- Contract administrator (F), Age 32, Massachusetts

■ ■ ■

It makes me happy …

When a psychic prediction comes true.

When a "blind date" is only blind to my shortcomings.

When my ex-girlfriend and I know
why we're no longer together.

-- Building sales representative (M), Age 50, California

■ ■ ■

It makes me happy ...

To finish the crossword puzzle in the newspaper.

To have brunch on Sunday
and not have to do the dishes.

To have my dog gallop up the stairs
to meet me in the morning ...

To win at Scrabble.

When my children go to someone else's house to play.

-- *Attorney (F), Age 48, Tennessee*

■ ■ ■

It makes me happy ...

When I wake up in the morning
and my hair's not in tangles.

When I finish my homework.

When my sister and I aren't fighting.

-- Student (F), Age 10, Maine

■ ■ ■

It makes me happy ...

To shop at Nordstrom's.

To watch "Unsolved Mysteries" on TV.

To Tsimshian (Indian dance!).

-- Executive secretary (F), Age 37, Alaska

■ ■ ■

It makes me happy ...

To make it through the entire aerobics tape!

When I don't burn the first pan of cookies.

-- Administrative secretary and mom, Age 31, North Dakota

■ ■ ■

What makes us happy?

When I can wear my high school size clothing --
10 years after graduation!

-- Assistant editor (F), Age 29, Missouri

■ ■ ■

Chowing down on a delicious Rhode Island clamcakes,
right before smoking a good cigar.

-- Governor's staff (M), Age 37, Rhode Island

It makes us happy ...

To occasionally see truth and justice triumph.

*-- Director of communications
with a dairy association (M), Age 60, Missouri*

■ ■ ■

To see my wife smile
and to see my Springer Spaniel run.

-- Insurance broker (M), Age 27, Utah

Things that make me happy ...

Being in front of a crowd at the podium and knowing --
they're mine -- and I am ON!

A good steak and a beer.

Life -- I wouldn't have missed this for anything!

*-- Association director of member
and government affairs (M), Age 47, Ohio*

■ ■ ■

It makes me happy ...

When the kids cooperate in the morning
and don't make me late for work.

When I have the answer
before my boss can finish the question.

When the kids on the football team call me "Mom."

-- *Executive assistant (F), Age 42, Alaska*

■ ■ ■

It makes me happy ...

When my wife fills my candy jar.

When I see my students do well in class.

When I win my bridge bid.

-- *Professor of Food Science (M), Age 57, Indiana*

■ ■ ■

Here are some things that make us happy ...

When I hear a child tell about an exciting adventure.

-- Ag journalist (F), Age 43, Colorado

■ ■ ■

When the phone does not ring
between 9 p.m. and 8 a.m.

-- Administrative assistant (F), Age 35, Georgia

What makes us happy?

To bring in the last load of hay just before the rain.

-- Dairyman (M), Age 60, Indiana

■ ■ ■

When my Mom, who has Alzheimer's,
knows me and my family. And when I get good,
big hugs from people who "know" how to hug.

-- Editor (F), Age 50, North Dakota

155

It makes me happy ...

When people appreciate me for who I am
and not for who they would like me to be.

When the underdog comes out on top.

When I find money in a jacket from last winter.

-- Healthcare administrator
and recent MBA graduate (M), Age 30, Washington

■ ■ ■

It makes me happy ...

When I see or hear about people of all races and ages
working together to clean up
our environment and our surroundings.

That I am able to touch people with my singing voice.

-- Receptionist (F), Age 26, New York

■ ■ ■

What makes me happy?

Sleeping in ... No appointments ...
Living in San Francisco ...
Having more than just enough money.

-- U.S. Postal Service letter carrier (M), Age 38, California

■ ■ ■

To see, anything and everything,
because two years ago my doctors told me
I could be blind within six months.

To know that even if I do lose my sight,
I will always have my memories
of how beautiful the world can be.

-- Educational psychologist (F), Age 34, North Carolina

■ ■ ■

What makes you happy?

If you'd like to participate in future volumes
of The America Says Book Series,
please contact us at:

The America Says Book Series
P.O. Box 40671
Nashville, TN 37204
FAX (615) 386-3959

OTHER TITLES BY GREAT QUOTATIONS PUBLISHING COMPANY

GREAT QUOTATIONS PUBLISHING CO.

1967 Quincy Court
Glendale Heights, IL 60139-2045
Phone (708) 582-2800
FAX (708) 582-2813